worried worried worried worried worried worried worried worried worried worried worried worried worried

worried worried worried worried worried worried worried worried worried worried

worried worried worried worried worried 我好擔心 worried

worried worried worried worried worried worried worried

worried worried worried worried worried worried

worried worried worried worried worried

Worried Worried Worried

RRIED 我好擔心 WORRIED

ORRIED

RRIED

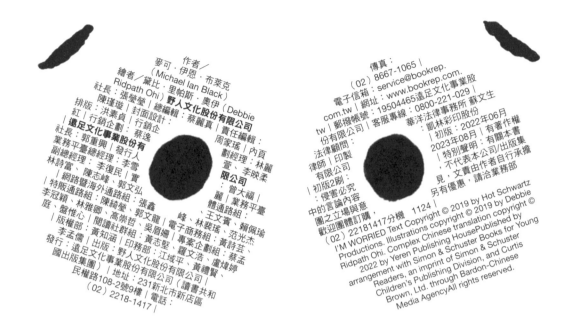

作者／麥可‧伊恩‧布萊克（Michael Ian Black）
繪者／黛比‧里帕斯‧奧伊（Debbie Ridpath Ohi）
社長：張瑩瑩｜總編輯：蔡麗真｜責任編輯：蔡逸
排版：洪素貞｜封面設計：蔡麗真
紅｜行銷企劃：林麗
野人文化有限公司
社長：郭重興｜發行人：李映柔
業務平臺總經理：李雪
副總經理：李復民｜實
林詩富、陳志峰、郭文弘
特販通路組：陳綺瑩、張鑫
李冠穎、林雅萱、高崇博、郭文龍
庭、盤惟心｜閱讀社群組：吳З娟、黃詩芸｜
版權部：黃知涵｜印務部：江域平、黃禮賢、
李孟儒｜出版：野人文化股份有限公司｜
發行：遠足文化事業股份有限公司（讀書共和
國出版集團）｜地址：231新北市新店區
民權路108-2號9樓｜電話：
（02）2218-1417｜

傳真：
（02）8667-1065｜
電子信箱：service@bookrep.com.
tw｜網址：www.遠足文化事業股
份有限公司｜郵撥帳號：19504465遠足文化事業股
份有限公司｜客服專線：0800-221-029｜
華洋法律事務所 蘇文生
律師｜印製：凱林彩印股份
有限公司｜初版：2022年06月
｜初版2刷：2023年08月｜有關本書
｜特別聲明：有關本書
中的言論與意見，文責由作者自行承擔
歡迎團體訂購，
（02）22181417分機　1124｜

獻給容易擔心的人：

現在，立刻，深呼吸，你沒事。

專注在當下。

—M. I. B.

獻給我親愛的朋友 Beckett。

你總是叫我別擔心，

這句話對我來說非常重要。

—D. R. O.

小野人48
我好擔心【中英雙語◆紐約時報暢銷作家超可愛繪本】
孩子的情緒認知四部曲(4)

作者／麥可‧伊恩‧布萊克（Michael Ian Black）

作家、諧星兼演員，曾參加《流金歲月》、《加菲根秀》、《哈啦夏令營：第一天》等電視
節目的演出。麥可定期在全美巡迴演出單人脫口秀，也著有暢銷書籍：《My Custom Van:
And 50 Other Mind-Blowing Essays That Will Blow Your Mind All Over Your Face》、
《You're Not Doing It Right: Tales of Marriage, Sex, Death, and Other Humiliations》；童
書包括《川普這種生物》（尖端出版）、《Chicken Cheeks》、《The Purple
Kangaroo》、《A Pig Parade Is a Terrible Idea》、《光屁屁小超人》以及《Cock-a-
Doodle-Doo-Bop!》。麥可與妻子及兩個孩子住在康乃狄克州。
官網：michaelianblack.com

繪者／黛比‧里帕斯‧奧伊（Debbie Ridpath Ohi）

童書作家及繪者，著有《誰偷走了我的書？》（野人文化出版），她曾與Simon & Schuster,
HarperCollins, Random House, Little Brown, Stone Bridge Press and Writer's Digest等出
版社合作，並為作家麥可‧伊恩‧布萊克（Michael Ian Black）《孩子的情緒認知繪本四部
曲》（野人文化出版）繪製插畫。
官網：DebbieOhi.com / Twitter: @inkyelbows/ Instagram: @inkygirl.

國家圖書館出版品預行編目(CIP)資料

我好擔心：孩子的情緒認知四部曲. 4 / 麥可‧伊恩‧布
萊克(Michael Ian Black)作；黛比‧里帕斯‧奧伊
(Debbie Ridpath Ohi)繪. -- 初版. -- 新北市：野人文化
股份有限公司出版：遠足文化事業股份有限公司發行,
2022.06
　面；　　公分. -- (小野人；48)
譯自：I'm worried(The I'm books)
ISBN 978-986-384-694-9(精裝)

1.CST: 生活教育 2.CST: 情緒教育 3.CST: 繪本

528.33　　　　　　　　　　　　　　　111003258

I'M
WORRIED
我好擔心

作者／麥可‧伊恩‧布萊克（Michael Ian Black）

繪者／黛比‧里帕斯‧奧伊（Debbie Ridpath Ohi）

野人

我好擔心。

I'm worried.

你在擔心什麼呢？

What are you worried about?

我擔心「未來」。

The future.

你為什麼擔心未來呢？

Why are you worried
about the future?

Because what
if something
BAD
happens?

因為我擔心會發生
不好的事……

你可以告訴我，
壞事永遠不會發生嗎？
拜託。

Please tell me
nothing bad will
ever happen.

馬鈴薯，我希望我可以，
但我沒辦法。

I wish I could, Potato,
but I can't.

因為沒有人知道未來會發生什麼事。
Because nobody knows
what's going to happen.

為什麼不可以？
WHY NOT???

嗯…我也開始擔心了。

Um, now I'M worried.

It's okay, you two.
Sometimes bad things happen.

你們別擔心。有時候，壞事就是會發生。

Like, Potato, remember that time
you rolled off the table?

比如說，馬鈴薯，記得有一次你從桌上滾下來嗎？

我瘀青了好幾個星期。

I was bruised for weeks.

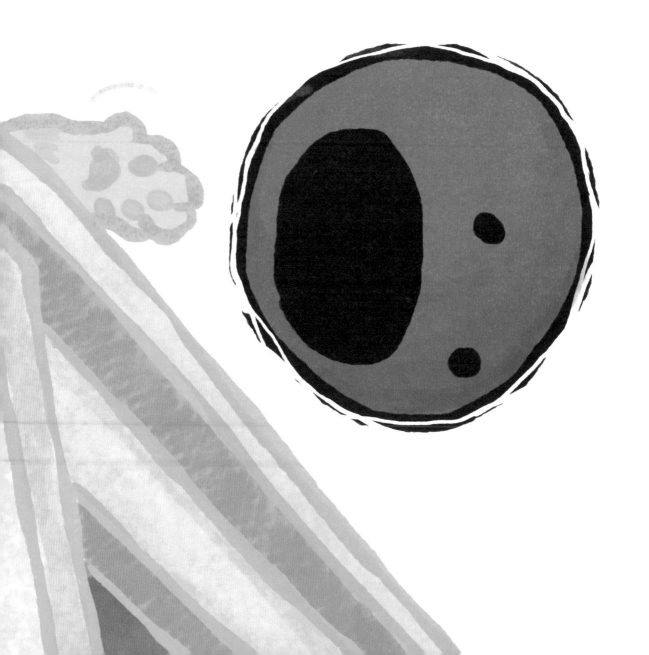

And, Flamingo, remember when
還有，紅鶴，記得

you got your beak stuck 你曾經嘴巴卡在
in the peanut butter jar? 花生醬罐子裡嗎？

Peanut butter is the worst.

都是花生醬害的。

And that time I fell off the monkey bars
and broke my arm?

還有，記得我從單槓摔下來那次，摔斷手臂嗎？

All of those things were bad at first...

這些事一開始都很糟...

I got a sticker at the
doctor's office and it was
scratch 'n' sniff!

醫生給我一張
**香香的
刮刮貼紙**！

我的三明治加了波隆那香腸，
更好吃！

I put bologna on my sandwich
and it was **delicious!**

You both doodled all over my cast
and it looked awesome!
你們還在我的石膏上塗鴉，
看起來超級棒！

I'm going to wrap
myself in
Bubble Wrap,
just in case.

我要用泡泡紙
把自己包起來，
以防萬一。

這樣就不會再有
壞事發生了！
That way nothing bad
can happen again!

Guys . . .
你們兩個…

你們…
Guys . . .

你們兩個？
guys?

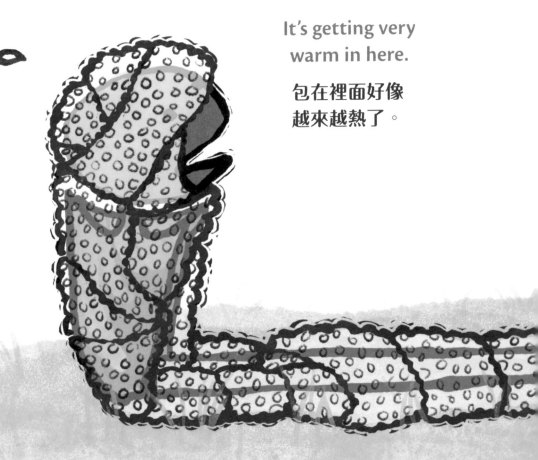

It's getting very
warm in here.

包在裡面好像
越來越熱了。

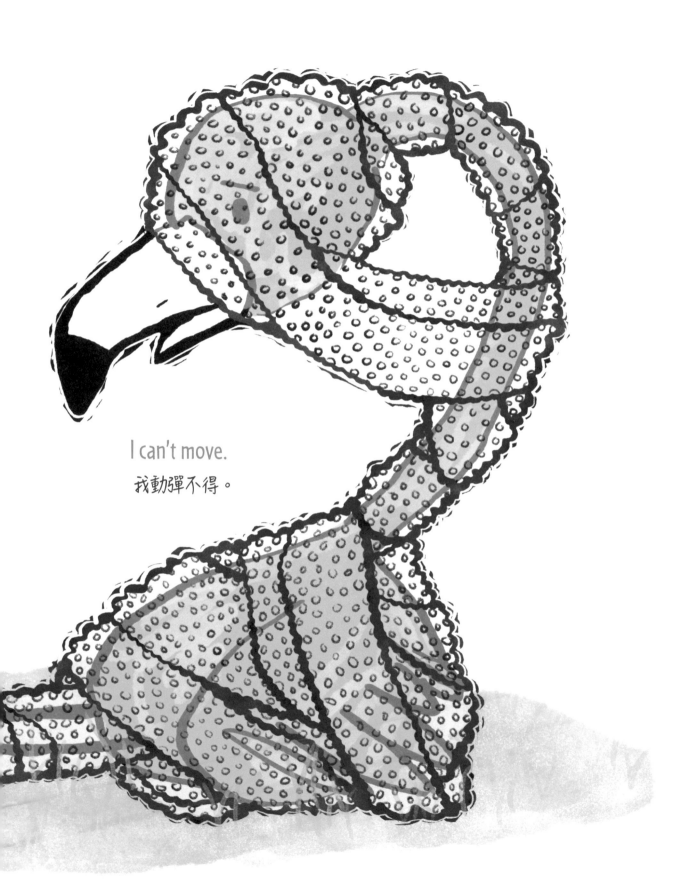

I can't move.

我動彈不得。

看吧？

See?

Worrying
doesn't help!

擔心也沒用！

既然不知道未來會發生什麼事，
我們就好好享受現在吧。

Since we don't know what's
going to happen in the future,
maybe we should just
enjoy the now.

享受「現在」？

Enjoy the now?

我這樣做對嗎？

Am I doing it right?

還不錯。

Yup.

棒透了！

You got it!

嘿，紅鶴。

Hey, Flamingo.

Yeah?

幹麼？

「享受現在」比
「擔心未來」還要棒多了！

Enjoying the now is
way better than
worrying about
the future!

(都是花生醬害的。) (But peanut butter is still the worst.)

worried worried worried worried worried worried worried worried worried worried worried worried worried wo

worried worried worried worried worried worried worried worried worried worried w

orried 我好擔心 worried worried worried worried worried wo

worried worried worried worried worried worrie

worried worried 我好擔心 worried wo

Worried Worried Worrie

WORRIED WORRIED WO

WORRIED W

WORRIED WORRIE

WOR